Bluestem Horizon

A Story of a Tallgrass Prairie

Dedicated with love to Bonnie Lee and Emily Lee, two young ladies who are as strong, beautiful and free-spirited as the flowers of the tallgrass prairie — E.B.L.

My love and thanks to J.T. and Jackie Z. for your ongoing support — K.B.

Book layout: Diane Hinze Kanzler
Editor: Judy Gitenstein

First Edition 1998
10 9 8 7 6 5 4 3 2
Printed in China

Acknowledgments:
   Our very special thanks to Bob Hamilton, Director of Science and Stewardship at the Tallgrass Prairie Preserve, Pawhuska, Oklahoma, for his curatorial review.

Library of Congress Cataloging-in-Publication Data

Lee, Evelyn.
   Bluestem horizon: a story of a tallgrass prairie / by Evelyn Lee;
   illustrated by Krista Brauckmann-Towns.
         p.   cm.
   Summary: While growing up on the tallgrass prairie, Young Bison and his three
   companions experience both a tornado which separates them from the herd and
   a prairie fire brought on by lightning.
      ISBN 1-56899-595-4 (hardcover)   ISBN 1-56899-596-2 (pbk.)
   1. Bison — Juvenile fiction.   [1. Bison — Fiction.   2. Prairies — Fiction.]
   I. Brauckmann-Towns, Krista, ill.   II. Title.
         PZ10.3.L514Se   1998   98-13739
         [E] — dc21   CIP
                                                                              AC

Bluestem Horizon

A Story of a Tallgrass Prairie

by Evelyn Lee

Illustrated by
Krista Brauckmann-Towns

Soundprints™
Where Children Discover...

One afternoon in late June, Young Bison, a yearling, moves with his herd through the tallgrass prairie, eating mouthfuls of big bluestem grass as he goes. Bright yellow flowers—coreopsis and prairie coneflower—speckle the open land that stretches as far as the eye can see. An eastern meadowlark zips past. Its call sounds like "see-you-see-yer." Dragonflies dart, grasshoppers feed, and a monarch butterfly flits from one butterfly milkweed plant to the next.

Under the hot sun, the bison move slowly. The grasses barely flutter, but across the vast prairie sky, clouds begin to gather, signaling another summer storm.

By late afternoon, clouds fill the sky. Gusts of wind ruffle Young Bison's fur and send the grasses into rolling waves. Lightning shatters the sky and thunder rumbles. The herd grows restless as the prairie sky turns a dark green.

Soon, hail pelts down, big as marbles, bouncing off the bison's heads and backs. The next instant, a black, funnel-shaped tornado can be seen on the horizon, swerving toward the herd. It is time to run!

As the winds circle furiously behind, Young Bison and the herd stampede. The ground shakes from pounding hooves. Badgers scurry underground. Northern bobwhite and red-winged blackbirds charge into flight. Nearby, a collared lizard presses itself into a sandstone crevice.

The powerful twister roars closer, ripping oak trees up by the roots. Branches hurtle past and tree trunks cross the herd's path. The bison race through the grass in every direction. Now, the hail turns to rain. Young Bison and three others veer down a ravine, galloping blindly. Then, finally, the violent tornado passes.

It is calm again. Tree branches litter the ground. Black-eyed susans and purple coneflowers lie trampled in the mud. A pocket gopher peeks out from its underground burrow then dashes back as a northern harrier soars overhead. A raccoon peeks from the safety of its den, and a greater prairie chicken scuttles through the grass.

Young Bison and the three other yearlings bellow, but there is no answer from the rest of the herd. The young ones are alone—for the first time ever.

The group searches for the herd. They move steadily over many miles, always grazing on their favorite summer foods—big bluestem and Indian grass.

Several days later, the group is walking single file on a dirt trail. Brown-headed cowbirds ride on their backs, pecking insects from their fur. Young Bison sees a dusty, hollowed-out bowl shape in the ground. It is a bison wallow, made recently by some older bulls from his herd.

He kneels, flops over, and slowly rolls back and forth to cover himself with dust. This rids him of more insects. The other bison take turns in the wallow, and then they move on.

Young Bison and the others wander for a whole week. All at once, Young Bison lifts his tail at full attention. He sees something moving through the prairie grasses!

It is only a coyote, stalking a jackrabbit. The group is safe, but they are still alone. Patiently, they plod on. As they come around an outcrop of rocks, Young Bison's keen sense of smell catches the scent of droppings from the herd. It tells him the other bison cannot be too far.

The scent of the other bison, getting stronger all the time, leads the small group to the crest of a hill. Away across the valley, deep in the basin, they see black dots scattered in the prairie grasses. They have found the herd!

Young Bison trots forward, followed by the other three. Several bison from the main herd bellow and plod toward them. They breathe into each others' faces with big snorts of welcome. The bison herd is together again.

Young Bison's mother has had a new calf. He now has a fuzzy, cinnamon-colored little sister!

By September, purple asters and arching goldenrod sway in the sea of late-summer green. Seedheads of big bluestem grass have grown so high Young Bison cannot see over them. Butterflies lay their eggs in plant stalks to wait for spring.

With another week's passing, scissor-tailed flycatchers and dickcissels leave the tallgrass prairie for warmer winter homes. A rough green snake settles into a protected hole and Young Bison's fur coat grows long and sleek.

Across the prairie, blades of bluestem grass turn golden-red and die, matted down to face the harsh winter ahead. Now, the bison find wild rye and sedges that grow green in the cooler season. They eat all they can, putting on weight for winter. They are joined by American goldfinches searching for thistle seeds and horned larks that will stay through the winter.

As Young Bison and the herd walk,
the drying grasses crackle under their hooves
and swish like paper in the autumn winds.
White-footed mice scamper through tunnels
of fallen bluestem, searching for coneflower seeds.
In the early autumn sky, red-tailed hawks circle
and dive, hunting for unwary mice that are too
busy storing food for winter. American tree
sparrows also scurry for the fall harvest. One day
a wild turkey, feasting on fallen acorns, scoots
away as Young Bison nears.

There are short afternoon storms, but the
rainwater dries quickly and the tallgrasses become
drier than ever.

Toward the end of September, a lightning storm sweeps the prairie. Jagged flashes brighten the sky and loud claps of thunder sound for miles. Suddenly, a bolt of lightning strikes the ground and orange flames shoot upward. The roots are safe underground, but the dried grasses burn hot and fast. The tallgrass prairie is on fire!

The herd runs, with smoke and flames following closely. As the frightened bison reach a stream, two white-tailed deer dart from the cottonwood shelter on the bank and leap the stream in two long bounds. This time, Young Bison follows his herd closely, plunging into the water as the fire sweeps to the branches of the cottonwood trees, and finally stops. On the opposite bank, the herd is safe.

As the days grow shorter and chillier, the large herd splits up. Young bulls form bachelor groups. Big, older bulls go off by themselves. Young Bison and his three companions stay in a small, mixed herd. His mother and her little calf are in another band with his older sister, who has a calf of her own.

In early December, Young Bison awakens to cold air and a light gray-colored sky. The world feels still. Fox squirrels, which were busier than usual gathering seeds the day before, stay in their nests. It can only mean one thing: Snow is coming to the prairie.

Flakes of snow begin to gather on their thick, dark coats. Young Bison and his herd turn head-first into the swirling snow. Puffs of steam billow from their nostrils in the frosty air. Together the bison will face the harsh winter. Together they will wait for the first green shoots of bluestem to poke out of the thawing earth. And together they will see the flowers bloom again, dotting their tallgrass prairie with a rainbow of color.

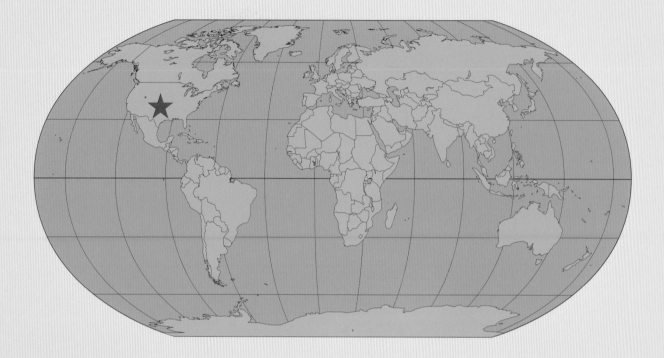

The Tallgrass Prairie Preserve, Oklahoma, United States

The Tallgrass Prairie Preserve is a protected area of 37,500 acres in
northeastern Oklahoma, owned and managed by The Nature Conservancy.
Grazing by bison is helping to bring back a habitat filled with hundreds of
species of plants and wildlife.

About the Tallgrass Prairie

I t is said that, before the 20th century, thirty to sixty million bison lived in North America's plains and prairie lands, which included the tallgrass prairie and, farther west, the midgrass and shortgrass prairies that spread to the Rocky Mountains. The tallgrass prairie alone covered 142 million acres, and stretched from Canada to the Gulf of Mexico, and from western Indiana to Nebraska.

By the late 1800s, hunters, settlers and the laying of the rail lines for the transcontinental railroad reduced the number of bison sharply. There were only a few scattered herds left. This small number dwindled even further as millions of acres of tallgrass prairie were plowed for croplands or used for grazing cattle. The tallgrass prairie habitat almost totally disappeared.

In 1989, The Nature Conservancy bought the historic Barnard Ranch—nearly 30,000 acres of unplowed prairie—as the first piece of the Tallgrass Prairie Preserve. The goal was to bring back the tallgrass prairie. In 1993 The Nature Conservancy let loose three hundred bison on the Tallgrass Prairie Preserve. By 1997 the herd had grown to six hundred fifty bison. It is The Nature Conservancy's hope to have 2,200 bison in the near future.

Each year, land managers carefully burn patches of the Tallgrass Prairie Preserve. Burning encourages new plants to grow and flower. New grass shoots that sprout after a fire are the bison's favorite food. While bison find these new grasses, other grasses and wildflowers grow undisturbed elsewhere in the Preserve. With this carefully balanced plan, the home of America's most ecologically and historically important mammal has been restored.

ADOPT A BISON! Be part of bringing back this great, wide-open tallgrass prairie. To find out how, call The Nature Conservancy's Oklahoma Field Office at (918) 585-1117.

Glossary

▲ *Black-eyed Susan*

▲ *Eastern meadowlark*

▲ *Red-tailed hawk*

▲ *Bur oak*

▲ *Fox squirrel*

▲ *Rough green snake*

▲ *Dragonfly*

▲ *Jackrabbit*

▲ *White-tailed deer*

▲ *Pale purple
coneflower*

▲ Bison

▲ Coyote

▲ Raccoon

▲ Big bluestem grass

▲ Greater prairie
chicken

▲ Sedge

▲ Eastern collared
lizard

▲ Heath aster

▲ Wild turkey